CV Resume Writing Techniques Get Hired Immediately

A comprehensive guide to write an eye-catching CV that gives lots of job interviews, with many employment getting tips

Smit Chacha

Copyright © 2019 Smit Chacha

All rights reserved.

ISBN: **9781073509812**

ACKNOWLEDGMENTS

I was 21 when I finished my University degree in Computer Visualization and Games. I was a freshman with no work experience in this field. I was looking for jobs in computer field, mainly games development, web design or 3d animation.

It was hard to get 1 interview; I remember those days when I use to apply for dozens of jobs every day. I have been to countless online job recruiters (Reed, Monster, Indeed, etc.) Also, in many Job Center Plus and career advisors such as: Seetec, YMCA and many others.

Been in many libraries not for reading books but to apply and to get advice in how to get in to the job market. It was taught but eventually I landed in my desired field.

Every time I visited the above places my CV was rewritten countless times, until I found how to write a perfect CV from employers' point of view. This took a lot of patients and hard work but eventually I started to get dozens of interviews. I found the secret of writing an interview winning CV.

Every time I used to apply for just a few jobs and would get 1 to 3 interviews a week. And this is what I want you to archive. I want you to get job interviews, I want you to learn how to write an interview winning CV. A CV that is written from employers' point of view.

In this book titled "CV Resume Writing Techniques Get

CV Resume Writing Techniques Get Hired Immediately
A comprehensive guide to write an eye-catching CV that gives lots of job interviews, with many employment getting tips

Hired Immediately" you will learn all the CV writing techniques that will guarantee you an interview. Plus, many interview winning techniques that you should know such as: how to prepare for an interview, how to do research before an interview, most common questions at an interview and how to answer them.

After reading this book you will be able to write you own CV from employers' point of view that will give you multiple job interviews a week. Results may vary; however, this book is based on my experience in how I got multiple interviews by learning how to write a perfect CV.

I also share with you on this book several ways in how to apply for jobs. Not only online but also by writing a cover letter and sending speculative letters.

Everybody asks me, "How do I write a catchy CV?" Thus, I decided to write this article. Here I will provide you useful information, including tips, in how to write a resume from the employer's point of view.

Writing a catchy CV may sound a bit daunting, however as you will see after reading this article that it is not that hard. Once you know what employers want to know when they see you CV everything starts to make sense. And this is what I am going to tell you!

You see, when you apply to a job (this can be via internet or via post) you generally tend you send some kind of details, that will prove that you are suitable for this job. And what are those details? Your CV of course!

So, you see, the employer knows you only from the CV, therefore you must write a very catchy CV, so that his or she can remember you! From my experience when the employer remembers you means that you are half way there! (Interview is coming soon).

So, how do I write a catchy CV?

You start you CV with a letterhead where you write your name, address and contact details.

Below the letterhead you write a very brief review (not more than 3 paragraphs longs) of what your CV is all about. Here you write what sort of work you are targeting, how many years of experience you have on that field and (if applicable) what qualifications do you in that field.

After the brief review you write your strengths/skills (in bullet points).

If you are a graduate then just below the skills you write the start and finish date of your course, including the degree name and the University name and address in capital letters.

After that you write your work experience, start dates and end dates the employers name and address. Also, your position and brief descriptions of your duties (no more than 3 paragraphs long).

We are almost done, after the work experience you write your hobbies and interests (do not skip this) - remember the employers only know you via your CV; this helps the employer to know what sort of person you are. Most people skip this area and as a result they lose their chances of getting an interview.

Lastly, you finish your letter stating that you are more than happy to provide good references of yourself upon employer's request.

C.V. or Curriculum Vitae is the most important piece of document when you are on the job market. With a high-quality C.V., you boost drastically your chances to get the job you desire! In this article I will give you 7 deadly rules in how to write an award-winning C.V.

The first rule of C.V. writing is to not exceed 2 pages; this gets really hard sometimes especially when you have lots of experience or qualifications.

The second rule is to always start your C.V. with a brief resume. In this area you will write a 2 to 3 paragraph long review about yourself. You will include your very latest qualifications, skills and the types of jobs that you are targeting. You will have briefly explained why these types are very suitable for you (backing up with your skills and qualifications).

The third rule is to list your qualification in a chronological order (very latest first). You will also mention the college name (in capital letters) and address along with the date of accomplishment.

The fourth rule if to list your skills in bullet points.

The fifth rule if to write the most closed match job experience that you had, chronologically (from latest first). You will include the name and address of the employer or company with your position and a sort description of your role. You should also include the month and year of starting and ending dates.

The sixth rule is to write about your interests and hobbies do not skip this rule. The employer knows you only from your C.V. so acknowledging these things helps them to figure out the kind of person you are (socially).

The seventh and the last rule is to reassure the reader that you can provide good references about yourself, by ending the document with "references available upon request".

In this article I will share 3 killer tips to improve your C.V. (curriculum vitae), as you know this little piece of paper is you ticket for getting that interview that you want. A good C.V. can drastically boost your chances for getting

CV Resume Writing Techniques Get Hired Immediately
A comprehensive guide to write an eye-catching CV that gives lots of job interviews, with many employment getting tips

that interview. In this article I will share 3 simple but powerful tips that will radically change the looks and feels of your current boring C.V.

Before I start let me tell you that C.V. can only give the interview but not the job, to get the job you need to pass the interview stage and that depends on you, on how you behave. Nonetheless most people do not even get a chance to get to an interview and if that is your case then this article is for you!

Here I will share 3 simple ways in how you can improve your current C.V. these 3 little changes are very simple to implement but very powerful as well! They will change the overall looks and feels of your curriculum vitae, so let's start:

#1 - Font, font size: the font and font size are very important, if you have your C.V. with big large fonts then it will make the reader fell that you are shouting and if you have very small font size then will make it fell very timid. In my experience the best font is: Areal, Times and Garamond and the size between 12 to 14.

#2 - Layout: the layout is extremely important; this makes your C.V. look profession and give you an impression of a very organized person. Create tables and

CV Resume Writing Techniques Get Hired Immediately
A comprehensive guide to write an eye-catching CV that gives lots of job interviews, with many employment getting tips

organic your C.V. data as follows: header, resume, skills, qualifications, experience, interest and references.

#3 - Style: style your C.V. meaning use the default table styles and stylize your C.V. this will really impact the looks and feels of your C.V.

C.V. or Curriculum Vitae is the most important document for job seekers. This short and simple document evaluates you from the employers prospective. In this article we will reveal the dirty secret behind the Job winning CV.

We will reveal 3 dirty tips that will boost your chances to your dream job!

Tip#1 create a 2/3 paragraph short Overview section on the top of your resume. In this section write 3 things only. They must be very brief and very direct. The things that you need to write in this section are:

Your knowledge (education degree as an example)

Your ambitions (the position you are applying for)

Your skills (your strengths that will impress the employers)

Tip#2 If you have a degree then create a box and write

the name of the degree and the date that it was awarded, followed by the Institution name (in capitals). If you do not have relevant qualification, do not worry instead of writing Educational details write your strength, your skills. Write in bullet points and then a 2-paragraph long description of real examples of using these skills.

Tip#3 always write your job experience with the latest date first and then go downward. If you do not have job experience, don't worry you can write your assignment or volunteer work that you have done.

And do not forget to double check your Curriculum Vitae for possible spelling or grammar errors!

Follow these killer tips and the job is yours!

CV is the curriculum vitae which is surely an important document that can land you in a perfect job. If you do not have a good and explicable C.V. then it becomes extremely hard to receive a job as per your wishes and strengths. It becomes most difficult when you do not hold the qualifications and experience in you.

A good C.V. always increases the probability to get the job or an interview. This is the reason that writing up a C.V. is significant.

CV Resume Writing Techniques Get Hired Immediately

A comprehensive guide to write an eye-catching CV that gives lots of job interviews, with many employment getting tips

Two aspects and objectives are important to write a C.V. zero qualification:

It is really important to expose your strengths and to minimize the chances of illustrating your weaknesses like zero qualification. The C.V. should be so impressive and readable that the person taking your interview gets attracted to it in single reading.

Focal Point

It is always claimed that the human eyes are attracted towards the focal point which is natural. The focal point is the one third down section from the top of the document. So, try to place all your important things and especially your strengths in this area. As per your thinking write it.

You should always give a second opinion to yourself if the first does not work well.

Presentation

If you are mature in your thinking and you are an objective applicant then it is not at all difficult for you to give a detailed explanation of your career history even if you do not possess a good qualification. Either the C.V. should be one page long or two pages long but never to be one and half a page document because it looks messy.

Thumb rules:

The C.V. should have whiter than the black for an easy reading.

Create a draft before transferring it into the actual C.V.

Never ever use the past tense.

Try to make use of short but sharp sentences that are free from any kind of jargon or waffles.

Employers normally use your CV as a means to shortlist people for interview and so it is essential that it promotes your best points. Employer is not looking into the spouse's capabilities. Employers often sum up potential candidates by reading the objective. The CV objective needs to demonstrate communication, leadership, future goals, and your ability to move forward in the work environment.

Employers take only a few seconds to decide whether or not you keep your CV, so you have to convince them quickly.

Include an objective up towards the top near where

CV Resume Writing Techniques Get Hired Immediately

A comprehensive guide to write an eye-catching CV that gives lots of job interviews, with many employment getting tips

you're going to include all of your contact information. You'll want to also include an academic objective so that it's really clear that you know what you're looking for and you can express that. Include specific skills, such as languages, administrative or computing skills, in a separate section in your CV. Then do not re-list them for every job you've used them in. Include details of each employer, dates of employment and your own job titles. Use concise sentences or bullet points to save space and ensure the document is aesthetically pleasing.

Recruiters reject CVs for any number of reasons, especially if poorly presented or contains basic errors. A poor impression makes recruiters consider wider employability issues as well as things like laziness and fundamental attention to detail, reading and writing skills, etc. Recruitment agencies will ask you for a CV so they can submit it to companies who are looking for your skills. Recruiters will judge your CV on how well you communicate, so choosing the right words, avoiding absolutely all grammar mistakes and spelling errors, etc. It is all about attitude!

A lot of people have no educational qualifications; however, this does not mean that they cannot find a job. You do not need qualifications to get a job; there are

CV Resume Writing Techniques Get Hired Immediately
A comprehensive guide to write an eye-catching CV that gives lots of job interviews, with many employment getting tips

hundreds of jobs out there that do not require any qualifications.

But how do I write my CV, if I have no qualifications?

A lot of people ask me this question and I answer them saying "but you have skills"! Everybody has skills! So do not be shy to write your skills on your CV and also remember that you are never too old to study or to learn new things. Able to read and write is itself a skill, able to communicate is also a skill not only that but also able to learn quickly is also a big skill. And I can go on and on...

So, you see qualifications is not everything, although having it facilitates a lot but that does not meant that you cannot find a job with no qualifications. And also remember that there is no age limit to learn. There are hundreds of free courses out there such as: basic IT, literacy, innumeracy, NVQ, etc.

Once you complete these free courses, they give a certificate which you can add on you CV. And many companies recognize these certificates.

Tip: If you having problems to find work because of lack of qualification then I suggest doing some volunteer work. Why? Because nowadays experience is more

CV Resume Writing Techniques Get Hired Immediately

A comprehensive guide to write an eye-catching CV that gives lots of job interviews, with many employment getting tips

important than qualifications. You will be surprised to know that many graduates cannot find work because of their lack of work experience. So, if you have work experience with you, does not matter if it is volunteer work, it will give you a huge advantage on this competitive job market, specially to someone with no qualifications.

Writing a good and effective CV, a CV that stands out from other competitive curriculum vitae takes loads of practice. But with if you follow these golden rules that I will show you on this article you will definitely boost your chances in getting an interview.

Below are the top 3 golden rules that you must follow to stand out your CV from other competitive CVs out there:

First golden rule: always write a profile on your CV. This profile must to exceed 4 paragraphs. In these 4 paragraphs you should write a very brief resume of what your CV is all about (do not forget to state the position you are targeting).

Second golden rule: use the most of the page; never leave a blank page, because a CV should never exceed 2 pages. A large CV is likely to go to the bin. Employers do not have the time to read every single page, so make use the most of your pages and remember do not exceed 2 pages.

Third golden rule: you should always write your education on the middle of the first page (especially if you are a graduate). If you are a graduate this must be your focal point of your CV, so writing on the middle of the first page will make it stand out. Formatting with some graphics is also advisable.

The best way to get a job interview is to write a good and catchy CV. With a CV like this you can really impress the employer and make them call you for an interview.

There are loads of job agencies that will charge you for writing an interview winner CV. In this article I will reveal the secrets or writing an interview winner CV (curriculum vitae). I will share you top 3 ways to write a catchy CV or resume.

Below are the top 3 ways to write a catchy CV that will impress employers:

Start the body of your CV with a good profile. A good profile never exceeds 4 paragraphs. In these 4 paragraphs you must write a very brief resume of what your CV is all about and also remember to tell the employer what type of jobs you are targeting.

CV Resume Writing Techniques Get Hired Immediately
A comprehensive guide to write an eye-catching CV that gives lots of job interviews, with many employment getting tips

If you are a graduate write your qualifications on the middle of the first page. This is your focal point of your CV. As this tells the employer that you have all the book and technical knowledge for the job that you are targeting.

Never ever exceed 2 pages when you write a CV. Employers do not like to read CV that exceed 2 pages. If they find a big CV, they are likely to throw them away. So, make the most of each page, try not to leave any empty space on your CV for this very reason.

So here you go, the top 3 ways to impress your employers with a good and catchy CV.

Although a good and catchy CV can help you to impress your employers. But you also require to write a good and catchy cover letter that will go with your CV.

A Curriculum Vita is the most important communication tool which gives the outlook of one educational career or a professional experience.

CV which is also known as the resume must be framed in such a way that it will provide great details in clarity with brief content. It is also necessary that information, listed in the CV should be written in a logical manner.

Good alignment and the margin will also make the CV to look well organized. The first step towards writing an effective CV is the collection of the various certificates, the history of employment and also the suitable references should be selected.

The next step is to make a good layout, select proper styles, it is well advisable to use times new roman font and font size to be 12. You can always feel free to have a look at the various CV's which are available in the internet to have a broad idea about the various contents.

The role of good CV becomes more important in increasing the chances of getting the interview call. The contents of the CV should be well written such that it will be easy for the employer to grasp all the details about you in a very short time; hence it is well advised that the content s of the CV should be brief and precise.

The large descriptions about the technical and also the educational experience of the person should be avoided and instead greater emphasis on the skills should be given to make the CV effective.

The format in which the CV is structured plays a crucial role in increasing the chances of the applicant to be called for the interview process. There is a great need that the applicant opts for the best CV format in order to match the expectation of the company members.

There are different kinds of the CV which are available each having its own share of merits and demerits. Depending on the current career situation of the applicant there will be one particular format which will best serve the purpose.

For example if a person is choosing to change the company, but wants to remain in the same field, then the chronological structure of the CV will be the best option.

In the other way around in which the person who is changing his field but persisting with the same kind of the job, then the reverse chronological order will be a good option.

There is a type of CV format called the functional CV which will be useful for all the people who are looking to change the direction completely, in this case the format of the CV will be mainly focusing on the achievements, skills and the organizational capability of the person and less importance to the job titles and experience.

There are also targeted and the alternative CV format to

help the talented person to apply in the design or other related industries. Hence there should be uncompromised level of the importance be given to the format of the CV. For a particular kind of the job, there will be one format of CV which will be the best.

A Curriculum Vita is the most important communication tool which gives the outlook of one educational career or a professional experience.

CV which is also known as the resume must be framed in such a way that it will provide great details in clarity with brief content. It is also necessary that information, listed in the CV should be written in a logical manner.

Good alignment and the margin will also make the CV to look well organized. The first step towards writing an effective CV is the collection of the various certificates, the history of employment and also the suitable references should be selected.

The next step is to make a good layout, select proper styles, it is well advisable to use times new roman font and font size to be 12. You can always feel free to have a look at the various CV's which are available in the internet to have a broad idea about the various contents.

CV Resume Writing Techniques Get Hired Immediately

A comprehensive guide to write an eye-catching CV that gives lots of job interviews, with many employment getting tips

The role of good CV becomes more important in increasing the chances of getting the interview call. The contents of the CV should be well written such that it will be easy for the employer to grasp all the details about you in a very short time; hence it is well advised that the content s of the CV should be brief and precise.

The large descriptions about the technical and also the educational experience of the person should be avoided and instead greater emphasis on the skills should be given to make the CV effective.

Curriculum vitae (CV) also known as the resume is considered to be the prime source which will help the applicant to seek an interview call. There is a great need that the various contents of the CV should be written with extreme care such that the profile of the applicant is rich enough to impress the employers.

Some of the key aspects which will help the person to achieve this goal include the proper listing of the various achievements and the skills possessed by you such that the employer will be convinced about your capabilities. The various responsibilities which the person has handled should also be mentioned with clarity such that the employer will be convinced that the applicant will be capable to handle the company issues.

CV Resume Writing Techniques Get Hired Immediately
A comprehensive guide to write an eye-catching CV that gives lots of job interviews, with many employment getting tips

It is also necessary to check the deadline for the application and to send the CV well in advance such that the employer will have enough time to read your CV fully and get impressed by it. The CV can also be made interesting with making the CV to appear in balance manner and also try to mention all the things in a positive manner.

The other useful tip to impress the employer is to use a good cover later which should be impressive at first look. The cover letter is also very significant aspect since it is the first of all the things which the employer gets to see to assess your CV.

Especially in today's competitive world, there is a great necessity to frame a CV to impress the employers to increase the chance of getting the interview call.

How to write a CV that will grab employer's attention

Many people ask me this question. So, I decided to write an article about this and reveal the secrets of writing the "interview winner CV".

In this article I will share 3 killer tips in how to write a perfect CV/resume

The golden rule of writing effective curriculum vitae is to

CV Resume Writing Techniques Get Hired Immediately

A comprehensive guide to write an eye-catching CV that gives lots of job interviews, with many employment getting tips

write it from the employer's point of view. Keeping that in mind, I have 3 killer tips that will help you to a resume that will stand out and grab the employer's attention.

Below are 3 golden tips that you must follow while writing your curriculum vitae:

1- Never exceed 2 pages; employers will throw your CV to the bin if they find a CV that exceeds 2 pages. So, make the full use of the page, do not leave any blank spaces on your CV.

2- Start your CV with a brief profile about yourself and also state what types of jobs you are targeting and justify why you think your skills are useful for those kinds of jobs.

3- On the last page, always write about your hobbies and interests. 1 paragraph is enough. Employers do not know anything about you. So writing about your hobbies and interests helps the employers to know more things about you.

So, there you go, 3 killer tips to write an interview winner CV. If you follow these tips that I just shared with you, you will boost your chances to receive a phone call from employers for an interview.

CV Resume Writing Techniques Get Hired Immediately

A comprehensive guide to write an eye-catching CV that gives lots of job interviews, with many employment getting tips

There are large numbers of common mistakes which are being made while writing the CV; this will have a very bad effect since it will spread a bad impression about the applicant. Some of the common mistake which people commit while writing the CV are listed in the following sentences.

There is a tendency for the applicant to send the same CV for all kinds of the jobs; this is a very bad practice since it each type of the job will require unique structure and the format of the CV such that it will be compatible. The other mistake is that people write long sentences and provide more descriptions about their technical experience, but this will spoil the effectiveness of the CV.

In some CV there will not be sufficient description about the expertise about the applicant and the contents of the CV will not be in such a way that it will target a particular kind of the role. Some applicant also makes errors in the grammars and the spelling, this will make the CV to look unprofessional.

The description of the education on the front page is also the other mistake; instead of this the more recent experience should be listed on the first page. Hence the applicant should be extra careful in avoiding these kinds

CV Resume Writing Techniques Get Hired Immediately
A comprehensive guide to write an eye-catching CV that gives lots of job interviews, with many employment getting tips

of the common mistakes. The above said tips to avoid the common mistakes if followed properly will surely help to improve the entire outlook of the CV such that it will surely impress the employer who reads through the CV.

Writing a cover letter can be a daunting task. But if you follow these instructions that I will show you in this article, writing a cover letter will not only be easy but enjoyable. I will share you with 7 killer tips that will grab the attention to the employers.

So, are you ready?

Always write a header on the cover letter, the header must have your name in capital letters following by your address and contact details. This information should always be written on the upper right corner of the page.

Follow your letter with the employers Name (with initiations abbreviations such as Mr. / Ms. or Mrs.), company name and address.

Never ever write your National Insurance number on a covering letter, not even on your CV (curriculum vitae).

Always date your letters in this format: "dd/mm/yyyy".

Start the body of the letter with the position you are

applying for. This is important because the employer may have more than 1 vacancy so they need to know which vacancy you are applying for. Formatting the text in bold is advised.

The first paragraph must not exceed 4 lines and in these 4 lines you must describe everything about yourself, this includes your skills, qualifications (if any) and the time span of the experience that you may have that is relevant for the job.

Always end the letter thanking the employer and ensuring them that they are free to contact you for more information about yourself.

Tip: Also try not write your birth date on the covering letter, unless the job application states you to write. Writing sensible information like this can lead to identity fraud.

The goal for writing a CV is not to get a job. A CV will never give you a job it will however a chance to get an interview.

And once you get an appointment for an interview then you can get job (depending how you perform obviously).

In this article I will show you how to write CV that will

CV Resume Writing Techniques Get Hired Immediately

A comprehensive guide to write an eye-catching CV that gives lots of job interviews, with many employment getting tips

stand out and impress the employers, improving your chances to get an interview.

If you follow these tips that I will share with you I guarantee that you improve your chances to get an interview.

Below are 3 simple but effective tips that will make you CV stand out:

You should always start the body of your CV with a brief introduction about yourself. It is advised that you also state what types of jobs you are targeting and why you think you are well suited for these types of jobs. But remember to be very brief (2/3 paragraphs is enough).

If you have good qualification, such as a degree write it on the middle of the first page. Formatting it is also advisable. Highlighting your strengths and qualification will impress and employers and improve your chances to get an interview. Studies have shown that putting content in the middle of the page grabs people attentions.

Never ever exceed 2 pages. Employers will never read CV that exceeds 2 pages, if they find a large CV, they are likely to throw them away.

CV Resume Writing Techniques Get Hired Immediately

A comprehensive guide to write an eye-catching CV that gives lots of job interviews, with many employment getting tips

Tip: Never ever write your birth date and your National Insurance number because this can lead in to identity fraud.

Below are the best ways to impress your employer during an interview. Follow these tips and succeed on your job prospects!

Your Composure

This begins with your dressing. Make sure you are looking tip top clean. If you are a man, your face should radiate brightness. Don't be too mean.

If you are lady, learn to put on a constant smiling face. This is a great tool to impressing your interviewer especially the male ones. Male interviewers are often time carried away by the way a lady appears. Remember the saying; "first impression matters". You may not get a second chance to correct the first impression. Hence be focused on your mission of getting the job.

Your approach to question asked

Take note of the following:

Be precise, straight to the point

Don't digress

CV Resume Writing Techniques Get Hired Immediately
A comprehensive guide to write an eye-catching CV that gives lots of job interviews, with many employment getting tips

Don't show you know it all, be humble

Don't rush to answer a question, take a little time to ruminate

Take deep breathe often and release your responses

Ask the interviewer necessary questions when due

Leave an impression behind.

No "Thank You Letter" afterwards

You don't need to write any "thank you" letter to the firm or directly to the interviewer. This may in fact terminate your appointment. It will seem you are coercing the company to employ you. Never try that!

Finally, be on the lookout for the result. Check your email and keep your phone on for the wonderful result you are expecting. Be positive and never give up! Follow the above tips and success is in your way!

In this article I will share with you the best ways to impress employer on an interview

If you want to be the winner in an interview, you have to put the following tips into consideration.

You must start with your appearance. Here is the ideal

dressing code for winners:

For the man:

You must be on your suit preferably black or blue colour with a white or blue packet shirt

Your necktie should be neat with a conservative pattern

Your shoes should be black and well-polished

Let your haircut be short preferably

No bears or moustaches. Keep trimmed to the least

No earrings

No heavy metals or coins in your pockets

For the ladies:

Be on your black suit with a jacket and a white top or blouse

Avoid the over high heeled shoes. Go for a good flat one that can give you freedom to walk

Long nails are not necessary, but if you must wear them, polish then to look attractive

You need only one set of moderate earrings

Avoid heavy perfume, make it lighter.

If you must be a winner, your response to questions asked should be precise. Learn to go straight to the point. Don't digress. Learn to take enough breathe before you answer. When in doubt be polite enough to acknowledge your ignorance of the question asked instead of giving the wrong answer.

In all, you must be a goal getter in all ramifications. Try and leave a good impression behind for your interviewer.

Below is a list of 8 common interview questions that you can always expect to be asked during an interview.

1 - Questions regarding who you are

Here you will be asked to introduce yourself and a little story about your life so far.

2 - Questions about your competence and strengths

Here the employer will like to know your ability to perform given tasks. He may also ask you to throw more light to the position you are seeking for.

3 - Questions concerning team work and bosses

Here your ability to work under instruction is examined. The employer will also try to find out whether you can work within a team.

4 - Questions about your knowledge of the organization

The employer in this segment will like to know how you come to know about their company.

5 - Questions regarding remuneration

Here, you will be asked the salary range you desire per month and how you want it paid.

6 - Ethical questions about stress and work

Here your attitude to work and stress is examined.

7 - Questions regarding your goals and objectives in life

Here, the interviewer will like to know your goal in life and where you are actually heading to. This is necessary, so that they will know which position you may be considered for.

8 - Questions for the interviewer

Here, the interviewer will normally ask whether you have some clarification or other questions for him.

In conclusion. There may be other questions you could

be asked to respond. The interviewer holds the key.

In this article I will share with some examples of winning answers you can use to do well in an interview. So, are you ready?

Let's use a typical example. Let's say you are a mechanical engineer with specialization in plant repairs and maintenance. Here are some questions you can expect and the tips for your answer:

Question 1: Tell me a little about yourself?

Tip for your answer: When responding to this request focus on both your personal and professional values that link to the job you are applying for. here is a typical answer you can give:

Answer: I'm an experienced mechanical engineer with extensive knowledge in plant repairs and maintenance. I have done a lot of work for many companies and individuals alike. I like working with people and preferring solutions to different aspects of plant maintenance.

Question 2: Who are you?

Tip for your response: You don't need to begin to tell

long stories about your life. What the interviewer wants is a very precise answer about yourself and why you are the best candidate for the job.

Answer: I'm Hilary, from Miami, a former mechanical engineering student of Harvard University. I am an experienced plant engineer who repairs and maintain various generators such as the one you have in your establishment.

In all, you have to employ winning strategy such as these above for answering interview's question. The bottom line is that you have to answer every question with focus to the particular job you are applying for.

Going for an interview is one of the serious events you can ever have in life. This is because; your future is tied to such it. If you succeed, you have a job to earn a living. Hence, you need to study carefully the various ways to prepare for such interviews. Here are some useful tips:

Get ready from home first.

You should begin the preparation from home. Package yourself well through the appropriate dressing code. Use more of black or blue suits with nice polished pair of shoes. Make sure you have a low cut if you are a man and a nice simple hairdo if you are a lady. As a lady; put on flat shoes that will give you balance when you stand before your interviewer. Avoid putting on gorgeous earrings. Just look simple, cute and neat. Above all, be at the venue at least 45 minutes to the commencement of the interview. This will give you ample time to get yourself composed for the interview.

Get prior information about the company

Never go into any interview on presumption. Make sure you have adequate pieces of information about the company and the post you are seeking for. Get information about how their products, their services, their team work modality, their salary scale and so on. This will help you know how to present your answers in a more focused way.

In all, be ready, confident and stay focused. Be positive and think positive. Do not let any negative thoughts come across you. Follow the above rules and the job is yours!

In this article I will share a list of perfect answers for your interview questions. So are you ready?

Below are 4 questions examples with possible best suited answers you can give in an interview.

CV Resume Writing Techniques Get Hired Immediately

A comprehensive guide to write an eye-catching CV that gives lots of job interviews, with many employment getting tips

General tips: Answers must link to the job you are applying for. Let's use a typical example. "I am John, from Florida searching for a job in an oil firm"

Question 1: Who are you?

Answer: I'm John Keller from Florida. I'm a mechanical engineering graduate with a flair to engine repairs and services.

Question 2: Why do you want this position?

Answer: I want the position because I want to contribute my quota to the growth of your company, for the good of your every increasing customer out there and for my own earning benefits.

Question 3: How has your education prepared you for this career?

Answer: I studied mechanical engineering in the Oxford University, London with an industrial training experience in Mobil Oil firm for 2 years.

Question 4: What level of Salary do you expect from this job?

Tip for response: Be very precise on this. You must have gathered enough current information on how much the company pay to their former and current staff. With that in mind choose an average amount of what the company pays. For instance, if they are paying $5000 to 10,000, you can make a choice of $7000.

In summary, the above are just sample question with answers. The main point you have to bear in mind is to answer every question by focusing on your area of specialization and on the post you actually want.

In this article I will share with you the secret in how to impress the employer on an interview.

Below are your wining secrets to impress your employer during an interview:

Make sure you appear very neat and tidy especially with regard to your dressing. This is the first area your interviewer will look at for impression.

How relevant are your answers to the questions asked? Do not go off point. Respond to questions directly with confidence.

Ask your interviewer questions when necessary. Some interviewers will always demand that to discover your level of intelligence quotient.

Maintain a friendly look. Don't be too mean. Lighten the

mood of your face and sit up facing the interviewer.

Control your nerves. Don't be tensed up. See the interviewer as a brother or sister you can relate with. One way to achieve this is to take deep breathe each time you feel tensed up. Breathe in enough air and then come down to tackle any posed question.

Know the technicalities of your area of specialization. Being a master in the area you are being interviewed gives you leverage over the rest. Hence, it is necessary for you to do your homework very well.

Make sure there is an impression you leave behind for your interviewer. This makes you to be remembered when the interviewer gets back to the boardroom for discussions with the management on who and who to be chosen.

In all, you must be a positive thinker. Visualize your success before the result comes out.

ABOUT THE AUTHOR

Smit Chacha is an author and a Bsc. Graduate with lots of experience in finding and getting jobs. He has been unemployed in the past and have successfully managed to many multiple employments with skills and techniques he learnt from Job Centre Plus, Seetec, YMCA and other employment centers.

After rewriting countless CV and Resumes and found

CV Resume Writing Techniques Get Hired Immediately
A comprehensive guide to write an eye-catching CV that gives lots of job interviews, with many employment getting tips

which type of curriculum vitae works best.

He also found many online and offline employment getting techniques with speculative letters and more.

This book is a comprehensive guide in how to get hired immediately! Follow the tips and guidelines and start working on your desired field.

www.ingramcontent.com/pod-product-compliance
Lightning Source LLC
Chambersburg PA
CBHW030737180526
45157CB00008BA/3215